WNBA
Young Stars

BY K. C. KELLEY

Chicago Sky star Diamond DeShields ▶

The Child's World®
childsworld.com

Published by The Child's World®
1980 Lookout Drive • Mankato, MN 56003-1705
800-599-READ • www.childsworld.com

Photographs
Cover: AP Images/Jevone Moore/Cal Sports Media.
Interior: AP Images: Thurman James/Cal Sports
Media 5, 17, 21; Aaron Lavinsky/Minneapolis Star
Tribune 9; Frank Franklin II 13; David Dennis/Icon
SW 14. Newscom: Jeffrey Brown/Icon SW 2, 10;
Rich von Biberstein/Icon SW 6, 18.

ISBN 9781503835344
LCCN 2019944747

Printed in the United States of America

Contents

Young . . . and Awesome!

Sports leagues always add new, young players. Some of them don't last. Some become stars. In the WNBA, new players join each summer from college. Other players arrive from other countries. Let's meet the best young players in the league right now. Which ones will become superstars? Who will lead their team to a championship? You have to watch the games to find out!

A'ja Wilson (right) was the 2018 WNBA Rookie of the Year. ▶

Ariel Atkins

Atkins had a dream season as a **rookie** in 2018. She helped the Washington Mystics reach the WNBA Finals for the first time. They didn't win. That makes her want to work hard to take the next step. In 2018, Atkins was one of the league leaders in **steals**. Before the 2019 season, she played for a team in Poland! Watch for Atkins to take the Mystics to the top.

Team: Washington Mystics

Height: 5'8" (1.78 m)

Position: Guard

College: Texas

Joined WNBA: 2018

Atkins uses her speed to drive to the hoop against the Atlanta Dream.

Napheesa Collier

Talk about a hot start! In 2019, in her first WNBA game, Collier scored 27 points! That was the second-most ever in a player's first game. Her scoring power helped the Minnesota Lynx to a lot of wins. Collier can do more than score. She is also a great **rebounder**. Her defense is excellent. Collier's coach calls her a "**Swiss Army knife**." Can Collier lead the Lynx army to victory?

Team: Minnesota Lynx

Height: 6'1" (1.85 m)

Position: Forward

College: Connecticut

Joined WNBA: 2019

Collier (in blue) is not afraid to dive after loose balls on the court! ▶

Diamond DeShields

DeShields added a new accessory for the 2019 WNBA season. Doctors told her to wear special contact lenses. Now she wears cool **goggles** over her eyes to protect the lenses. In an early 2019 game, she poured in 21 points! Good eye! DeShields comes from a sports family. Her dad, Delino, played for several big-league baseball teams. Her brother, Delino Jr., is with the Texas Rangers. Keep your eyes on Diamond as a future star!

Team: Chicago Sky
Height: 6'1" (1.85 m)
Position: Guard
College: Tennessee
Joined WNBA: 2018

Like her speedy dad, DeShields can flash past defenders.

Asia Durr

How much did Louisville fans love Asia Durr? Hundreds of them drove to watch her play in 2019. In college at Louisville, Durr was an **All-American** twice. Fans from there made the trip to see her play in the WNBA! Durr was the second pick of the 2019 WNBA Draft. She quickly became a **starter** for the New York Liberty. She hopes to make her new Liberty fans just as happy!

Team: New York Liberty

Height: 5'10" (1.78 m)

Position: Guard

College: Louisville

Joined WNBA: 2019

Durr leaps over a defender to attack the basket. ▶

Allisha Gray

Allisha Gray is used to winning. In high school, she led her team to a state championship. At the University of South Carolina, she was a national champion. In her first pro season, she helped the Dallas Wings reach the playoffs. Plus, she won the 2017 WNBA Rookie of the Year award. Dallas had a losing record in 2018. That just gives Gray more reason to work hard to get back to the top!

Team: Dallas Wings

Height: 6'0" (1.83 m)

Position: Guard

College: South Carolina

Joined WNBA: 2017

◀ Gray is an all-around star. She can shoot well, pass the ball, and play solid defense.

Kelsey Plum

In college, Kelsey Plum was a powerhouse. She set the national record for most points scored in a season. She also set the **career** scoring record! No surprise that she was the No. 1 overall WNBA Draft pick in 2017. She joined the San Antonio Stars. In 2018, that teamed moved and became the Las Vegas Aces. Plum's all-around game is certainly aces! She also played for the US national team that won the World Cup in 2018!

Team:
Las Vegas Aces

Height: 5'8" (1.73 m)

Position: Guard

College: Washington

Joined WNBA: 2017

Plum is one of the best outside shooters in the WNBA. ▶

Brittney Sykes

Sykes has poured in a lot of points for the Atlanta Dream. She joined the team in 2017 after setting scoring records in college. In 2019, she scored points of another kind. In a video that went viral, she gave a young fan a pair of sneakers. The fan was so excited! If Sykes keeps scoring, maybe that fan can cheer for a champion!

Team: Atlanta Dream

Height: 5'9" (1.75 m)

Position: Guard

College: Syracuse

Joined WNBA: 2017

In a 2017 game, Sykes scored 33 points, her personal WNBA best.

A'ja Wilson

Wilson was named the college Player of the Year in 2018. Soon after, the Aces made her the No. 1 pick in 2018. Good choice! She poured in points and grabbed a ton of rebounds. She was the WNBA Rookie of the Year. She led the league in **free throws** made, too. Wilson is a strong player. She can push to the basket and score often. After the 2018 season, she played for a team in China. She came back to lead the Aces in 2019.

Team:
Las Vegas Aces

Height: 6'4" (1.93 m)

Position: Forward

College: South Carolina

Joined WNBA: 2018

Wilson is always trouble for the other team near the basket. ▶

Glossary

All-American (ALL-uh-MARE-ih-kan) a member of a group voted as the best in the country in a college sport

career (kuh-REER) the length of a person's time in a job, in a sport, or in college

free throws (FREE THROWZ) shots after a player is fouled, taken from a line 15 feet (4.6 m) from the basket

goggles (GOG-ullz) large plastic eye coverings often worn by athletes

rebounder (REE-bownd-er) a basketball player who grabs missed shots

rookie (RUH-kee) a player in her first season as a pro athlete

starter (START-er) a player who begins the game on the court instead of the bench

steals (STEELZ) in basketball, when a defender knocks away the ball from an opponent and recovers it

Swiss Army knife (SWISS AR-mee NYF) a type of knife that has many blades and tools; in sports, a player who can do many things well

Find Out More

IN THE LIBRARY

Buckley, James Jr. *It's a Numbers Game: Basketball*. Washington, DC: National Geographic Kids, 2020.

Macy, Sue. *Basketball Belles: How Two Teams and One Scrappy Player Put Women's Hoops on the Map*. New York, NY: Holiday House, 2019.

Sports Illustrated Kids. *My First Book of Basketball*. New York, NY: Sports Illustrated Kids, 2018.

ON THE WEB

Visit our Web site for links about the WNBA:
childsworld.com/links

Note to Parents, Teachers, and Librarians:
We routinely verify our Web links to make sure they are safe
and active sites. So encourage your readers to check them out!

Index

About the Author

K.C. Kelley is the author of more than 50 books on sports for young readers, as well as many sports biographies. He lives in Santa Barbara, California.